The BiG Book of HaPPY

Packed with **notes** to **tear** and **share!**

Published by American Girl Publishing
Copyright © 2012 by American Girl

Questions or comments? Call 1-800-845-0005,
visit **americangirl.com**, or write to Customer Service,
American Girl, 8400 Fairway Place, Middleton, WI 53562-0497.

Printed in China
12 13 14 15 16 17 18 LEO 10 9 8 7 6 5 4 3 2 1

Editorial Development: Trula Magruder
Art Direction & Design: Lisa Wilber
Production: Tami Kepler, Sarah Boecher, Jeannette Bailey, Judith Lary,
Jolene Schulz, and Jessica Rogers

Photography: cover—iStockphoto/Salihguler (dog and cat);
p. 3—iStockphoto/GlobalP (peacock)

Illustrations: p. 1—iStockphoto/minimil (elephant)

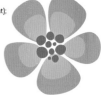

ear Reader,

hog-wild handing out hilarious and heartfelt messages
family and friends. **Hound** your pals with posters of
aise. Get your grandma's **goat** with jolly jokes. **Pony** up
eer cards for classmates.

e delightful **dogs,** crazy **cats,** kooky **cows,** and other
orable **animals** will deliver the perfect message to
meone who needs a little sunshine in her day.

fish around for just the right page, fill in the "To" and
om" on the back, and pass it on. Then *you'll* feel as
oud as a **peacock!**

our Friends at American Girl

To: ....

From: ....

Whoopee!

**Today's temperature is
snowball-fights-on-sledding-hills degrees.**

To: ....

From: ....

This card entitles you to

a wish.

To: ....

From: ....

Smart is so cool.

To: ....

From: ....

Circle of Friends

Are we two peas in a pod or opposites who attract?

- Chapter books
- Comic books
- Do-it-yourself books
- Coloring books

Find out! Circle your favorite, and I'll circle mine.

To: ....

From: ....

Have a **splash-happy** day!

To: ....

From: ....

To: ....

From: ....

Use your noodle,
and start your day with a smile.

To: ....

From: ....

To: ....

From: ....

Illustration: Carol Yoshizumi

Make today a **model** day!

To: ....

From: ....

I'm really happy today because

To: ....

From: ....

You can never have too many
Friends!

To: ....

From: ....

I'm so happy that I feel like singing! Here's why:

....

....

....

....

....

....

....

....

....

....

To: ....

From: ....

Have a happy

half-birthday!

To: ....

From: ....

To: ....

From: ....

To: ....

From: ....

To: ....

From: ....

**Here's my idea of
a perfect sleepover:**

Theme: ....

....

Food: ....

....

Craft: ....

....

Game: ....

....

Wanna join me?

To: ....

From: ....

This may be a stretch,

but you **ALWAYS** make me smile.

To: ....

From: ....

**Return this coupon,
and one argument between
you and me will end.**

To: ....

From: ....

Sorry you're sad.

I hope this smile brightens your day.

To: ....

From: ....

Laugh & pass

Why shouldn't you tell pigs secrets?

Because they'll squeal!

To: ....

From: ....

Need help with Internet research?

Return this coupon, and I'll MIH
(Make It Happen).

To: ....

From: ....

To: ....

From: ....

UR1DRFL

To: ....

From: ....

Want to go play?

To: ....

From: ....

You're
back!

I've
missed
you
so much.

To: ....

From: ....

Have an
egg-citing
morning!

To: ....

From: ....

Bravery comes in all SHAPES and sizes.

To: ....

From: ....

Here are some of the highlights you've missed.

Class assignments: ....

....

....

News: ....

....

....

Other stuff: ....

....

....

To: ....

From: ....

Need a **favor** from me?

Return this coupon.

To: ....

From: ....

THANK YOU
very much.

To: ....

From: ....

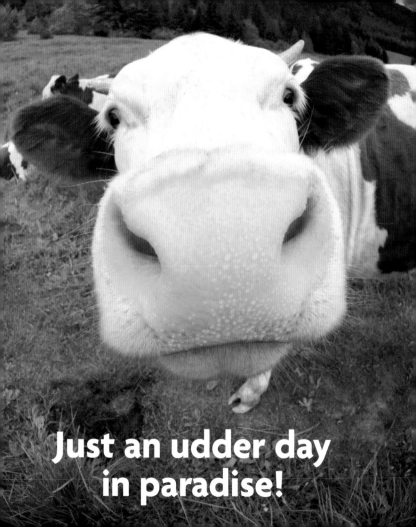

Just an udder day in paradise!

To: ....

From: ....

You're my
cup of tea.

To: ....

From: ....

Sometimes we
just need
to get out
and play.

Are you ready?

To: ....

From: ....

This coupon gives you

permission to relax!

To: ....

From: ....

Let's color!

To: ....

From: ....

I'm sooooooo

glad we met.

To: ....

From: ....

Sometimes you just need to **laugh** at yourself.

To: ....

From: ....

Look at things in a new way.

It can make the ordinary

extraordinary!

To: :...

From: :...

Take note!

Let's meet.
Ewe name the place.

To: ....

From: ....

Sometimes I feel like **you**

are the only one I can talk to.

To: ....

From: ....

To: ....

From: ....

Tuck Lucky inside your pocket, and you'll finish the day on top.

To: ....

From: ....

Circle of Friends

Are we two peas in a pod or opposites who attract?

- Drinking hot cocoa by a fireplace
- Snowboarding
- Skiing
- Ice skating

Find out! Circle your favorite, and I'll circle mine.

To: ....

From: ....

Illustrations: Stacy Peterson, Lisa WIlber

BE YOURSELF.

(Besides, everyone else is taken!)

To: ....

From: ....

You may be going solo today,

but I'll be with you in my

heart.

To: ....

From: ....

You are who you are,

and I love you for that.

To: ....

From: ....

Be a collector of good days.

Here's one now!

To: ....

From: ....

You are **beary** cute today.

To: ....

From: ....

Why do hens
lay eggs?

If they threw
them, the eggs
would break!

To: ....

From: ....

To: ....

From: ....

The top **5** things that make me smile:

1. ....

2. ....

3. ....

4. ....

5. This picture!

To: ....

From: ....

Here's the latest
buzz . . .

....

....

....

....

....

....

To: ....

From: ....

Return this coupon,

and I'll help with your homework!

To: ....

From: ....

Happiness is finding your own style.

To: ....

From: ....

You are
snow cute!

To: ....

From: ....

Circle of Friends

Are we two peas in a pod or opposites who attract?

- Biking
- Hiking
- Walking
- Reading

Find out! Circle your favorite, and I'll circle mine.

To: ....

From: ....

Friends sprinkle happiness into life.

To: ....

From: ....

To: ....

From: ....

You're going to **love** reading this book:

· ·

· ·

· ·

To: ....

From: ....

I'm so **happy**

that we are in this world at the same time.

To: ....

From: ....

You're not gonna believe this.

....

....

....

....

....

....

....

....

....

To: ....

From: ....

Because you're a **hoot,**

you get to pick the game
at recess today.

To: ....

From: ....

To: ....

From: ....

Snake Break

**Present this coupon,
and I'll help you practice**

a sssport,

a ssspeech,

or a sssong.

To: ....

From: ....

Illustration: Stacy Peterson

Happiness is being grateful for those who matter

. . . like you.

To: ....

From: ....

Hip,
hop,
hooray!

You were
very **special**
today.

To: ....

From: ....

Something to Celebrate

Be grateful that today is Saturday.
It means you still have tomorrow
to monkey around.

To: ....

From: ....

I know you've been feeling low recently, so I wanted to cheer you up. Here's what I plan to do:

....

....

....

....

....

To: ....

From: ....

To: ....

From: ....

Did you know . . .

I think you are

really

wise.

To: ....

From: ....

Let your signature
be a smile.

To: ....

From: ....

A team is a powerful thing.

I'm glad you're on mine.

To: ....

From: ....

Something to Celebrate

Be grateful that today is Sunday.
It means you can slow down
and notice what's really
important to you.

To: ....

From: ....

Happiness works like a mirror.

When you're happy, you may make others feel happy, too.

To: ....

From: ....

Which animal always likes to have a good time?

The dolfun!

To: ....

From: ....

I'm so **glad**

I met someone who's just like me.

To: ....

From: ....

Neighbor, we like you. And we like snow.

So Mom said to tell you how doggone
excited we are to shovel your sidewalk.

To: ....

From: ....

Here's the math problem I'm working on now:

Smarts
Spirit
+ Sweetness
YOU

To: ....

From: ....

A **smile** is understood all over the world.

To: ....

From: ....

Three cheers for family night!

To: ....

From: ....

To: ....

From: ....

Thanking you in English isn't enough.
So here's a Japanese thank-you, too.

To: ....

From: ....

Uh-oh!

I feel a laugh attack coming on.

To: ....

From: ....

I know you're new here,
so I'm giving you my number

in case you have any questions or
need a friend: ....

To: ....

From: ....

I really look up to you. Thanks for that.

To: ....

From: ....

This coupon entitles you
to borrow any book
from my collection.

Choose
one!

To: ....

From: ....

Together

is a wonderful place to be.

To: ....

From: ....

MOOD METER

How are you today?

Circle one.

Grr-eat   Grr-ouchy

1   2   3   4   5

To: ....

From: ....

Don't worry.

You'll be great!

To: ....

From: ....

Being with you
is the **purrfect** way
to spend the day.

To: ....

From: ....

HEY!
I'm *always* here
if you want
to talk.

To: ....

From: ....

You make
everything
better.

To: ....

From: ....

I need a pep-talk partner.
Will you be mine?

To: ....

From: ....

To: ....

From: ....

Illustration: Jenn Skelley Duval

(whatever the weather)

May your day∧be filled with

sunshine!

To: ....

From: ....

To: ....

From: ....

Take note!

I just saw something
very cool.

....

....

....

....

....

....

....

To: ....

From: ....

THANK YOU

for believing in me.

To: ....

From: ....

I had an **extra smile,**

so I'm giving one to you.

To: ....

From: ....

You can always
lean on me.

To: ....

From: ....

You look FABULOUS, dahling!

To: ....

From: ....

Why are frogs always happy?

Because they *eat* **bugs** whatever them.

To: ....

From: ....

no one understands me

BETTER THAN YOU DO.

To: ....

From: ....

Thinking of you
is my
**favorite
thing**
to do.

To: ....

From: ....

To: ....

From: ....

Snap!

You are picture-perfect.

To: ....

From: ....

Congratulations on your graduation!

I guess this makes you
THE SMART ONE.

To: ....

From: ....

THANK YOU
FOR YOUR KINDNESS.

To: ....

From: ....

Happiness

is traveling with a fun friend.

To: ....

From: ....

I may seem prickly on the outside,

but on the inside,
I'm soft and sweet.

To: ....

From: ....

To: ....

From: ....

Now that we're together,
I am
beary happy.

To: ....

From: ....

Today's temperature is running-on-the-beach-with-your-best-friend degrees.

To: ....

From: ....

Life is full of little adventures.

Want to share one?

To: ....

From: ....

You made me what I am today—

happy!

To: ....

From: ....

We're going
to have fun.
Want to come along?

To: ....

From: ....

You are a

VIP

to me

—a Very Important Pal!

To: ....

From: ....

Color me *happy* today!

To: ....

From: ....

To: ....

From: ....

You like to **boogie** and I like to **woogie**,
so let's invent a boogie-woogie dance.

Our dance title:

....

To: ....

From: ....

You give
the
best
hugs.

To: ....

From: ....

I'm just **hanging out** waiting for you!

To: ....

From: ....

You are 100% lovable.

To: ....

From: ....

What kind of tales do rabbits like best?

Stories with **hoppy** endings

To: ....

From: ....

Want to
stick
around?

To: ....

From: ....

Don't worry.
I'll wait
right here
until I see
you again.

To: ....

From: ....

Your friendship makes me
bubble over
with joy!

To: ....

From: ....

Friends add
harmony
to your life.

To: ....

From: ....

Circle of Friends

Are we two peas in a pod or opposites who attract?

- Swimming in the ocean
- Floating on a pool toy
- Scuba diving
- Snorkeling

Find out! Circle your favorite, and I'll circle mine.

To: ....

From: ....

Illustrations: Stacy Peterson, Lisa WIlber

Did you know?

I love you.

To: ....

From: ....

Having a happy moment?

Tell us about it!

Send letters to

The Big Book of Happy Editor
American Girl
8400 Fairway Place
Middleton, WI 53562

Photos can't be returned. All comments and suggestions received by American Girl may be used without compensation or acknowledgment.

Here are some other American Girl books you might like:

❑ I read it.

❑ I read it.

❑ I read it.

❑ I read it.